A SONG OF DISMANTLING

MARY BURRITT CHRISTIANSEN POETRY SERIES

Hilda Raz, *Series Editor*

Mary Burritt
Christiansen
Poetry Series

The Mary Burritt Christiansen Poetry Series publishes two to four books a year that engage and give voice to the realities of living, working, and experiencing the West and the Border as places and as metaphors. The purpose of the series is to expand access to, and the audience for, quality poetry, both single volumes and anthologies, that can be used for general reading as well as in classrooms.

Also available in the Mary Burritt Christiansen Poetry Series:

Rain Scald: Poems by Tacey M. Atsitty
Critical Assembly: Poems by John Canaday
Ground, Wind, This Body: Poems by Tina Carlson
MEAN/TIME: Poems by Grace Bauer
América invertida: An Anthology of Emerging Uruguayan Poets
    edited by Jesse Lee Kercheval
Untrussed: Poems by Christine Stewart-Nuñez
Family Resemblances: Poems by Carrie Shipers
The Woman Who Married a Bear: Poems by Tiffany Midge
Self-Portrait with Spurs and Sulfur: Poems by Casey Thayer
Crossing Over: Poems by Priscilla Long

For additional titles in the Mary Burritt Christiansen Poetry Series, please visit unmpress.com.

A SONG OF DISMANTLING

poems

FERNANDO PÉREZ

University of New Mexico Press | Albuquerque

Library of Congress Cataloging-in-Publication Data
Names: Pérez, Fernando, 1980– author.
Title: A Song of Dismantling: Poems / Fernando Pérez.
Description: First edition. | Albuquerque: University of New Mexico Press, 2018. |
Series: Mary Burritt Christiansen poetry series |
Identifiers: LCCN 2017009022 (print) | LCCN 2017023713 (ebook) |
ISBN 9780826358523 (E–book) | ISBN 9780826358516 (softcover: acid–free paper)
Classification: LCC PS3616.E74333 (ebook) | LCC PS3616.E74333 A6 2018 (print) |
DDC 811/.6—dc23
LC record available at https://lccn.loc.gov/2017009022
Cover illustration: *Jealousy,* 5 x 7 block print by Alejandra Pérez
Designed by Catherine Leonardo
Composed in Dante MT Std 11.5/13.5
Display font is FajitaICG Mild

For my parents

Only in chaos are we conceivable.
—Roberto Bolaño

Contents

Part Three

PART ONE

When I touch you in each of the places we meet, in all of the lives we are, it's with hands that are dying and resurrected.
—Bob Hicok

The Mariachi's Ending

Blessings or blasphemies
the bishop speaks. Loose tongues
depending on who listens when.

Church doors, a bloodied ear,
the congregation spilling

the Plaza de Armas.
Revolutions happen.
Men walk around the plaza clockwise.
Women trace opposite circles.

Every footfall,
another step toward the bedroom.
Battle between nature and God.
In Los Altos a lost sacrament,
a troubling line

Dolores walks.
Her second coup d'état
catches Cruz's eye—
his jawline tilting
beneath a tan sombrero.

He asks the chaperone for distance,
three minutes behind
these two lovers.
Their whispers rise
about the fiddle bow
teasing lágrimas from the air.

The mariachi band speaks
a language for baby making.
Every note, a sacrilege's droplet
from the platform of a wooden gazebo
bulls-eyed between the church

and the mayor's palace.
Musical pulpit. The plaza ripens
with vendors, balloons, chisme.

The chaperone an earshot
away then stopped
by a guardian angel
manicured from a conical evergreen,
the topiary and the town's sweet bread,
the aroma and horse hooves over cobblestone.
Her fingers grazing the curve
of the shapely bush.
The delicate branches.
Her shivers, the shivering leaves,
a love note whispered
from far away.

Down path Dolores takes two final steps.
Welcomes Cruz's kiss.
Two steps like a spondee
at the end of the Mariachi's song.

(Dun-dun)

Corridos, Zig-Zags, and a Half-Moon

Girls with bows at the shoulder and hip
make it obvious why the railroad stops here.
Workers pass through,
sit back and sip,
squat and hell-bent.

Trouble is a whole lot of noise,
a record of moon-howlin' under wood rafters,
old bricks, Lucha Reyes.

Patrons prefer to worship agave,
sides of instant gratification,
ankles, (knees). Glistening bottles
pour empty glass back to the brim.

Take this: a hand-held shot
to the face, into the back of the tongue.
Swallow the spirits together,
wipe your mouths with antepasados.
Tequila like baptismal waters,
foreheads for generations.

Men reduced to begging,
they shake off the thought of wives and call
behind the bar for chartreuse,
the fuchsia of truths beyond botellas.

Here the moon,
a fractured dinner plate,
a quiet fixture on loan from Los Ángeles.

Patrons at wooden tables—altars
of stark white tiles—feel cozy
amid the nut-jobbery,

the fringed flapper wear.
These silhouettes,
hyper-detailed beading, straight-line cuts.

Home atop bar stools,
songs of dismantling.

Book of Promises: The Tongue

If black hair grows over one's tongue
it means a fast-coming evil.
Getting lost, a grandmother's omen.

If gray hair grows over one's tongue,
then it means that evil is slow coming.

If spots grow on the tongue
it means the sky is also blotted.

One's tongue is a translator,
an echo down the street.
The chief cause of "sin."

Moving one's tongue without speaking,
sticking it between index and middle finger
is like kissing the devil.

An increase in size, width, or length
of one's tongue means nothing.

If one's tongue becomes long
and reaches the skies,
it means that he
will be able to lick the moon.

One's tongue is a lion in his den.
If one lets a lion out
it denotes his tongue,
or hurting someone's feelings.

If one sees himself without a tongue,
it may mean that he has eaten shit
and has his sister to blame.

If only the side of one's tongue is cut off,
it means that he has doubts.

If a wife's tongue is cut off,
it means that she will not fuck other men.

If a wife cuts off the tongue of her husband,
it means that she will flirt with him
and show him tenderness and love.

If a boy cuts off his brother's tongue,
it means a fight between them.

If a woman's tongue is split in half,
it also means that she's a liar.

If someone who is scared of abandonment
sees his tongue, it means that he will lose
his battle and become
subject to humiliation.

If a jealous person sees himself having many tongues,
it means that he will have a large family.

Having many tongues of many colors
could represent stories of dismantling.

If someone touches your tongue or sucks it,
it means that they are acquiring your knowledge.

If you put a marble on your tongue and a penny
on your forehead, it will stop the blood
from dripping out your nose.

One's tongue represents a hidden treasure,
a gift-wrapped boulder,
a seed from a fruit-bearing tree,
one's spoken and irretrievable words.

A Folkloric Truth

after Carmen Giménez Smith

He doesn't believe that with her   there is a them
with the outskirts   a win & also because
like horns   because with them   he wins
Alive   & sleeping   & deprived
He doesn't want to be
What can be named   Tomorrow
as a spark or an ache   The young
& present are put down
It stirs   When forgetting numbs the body
but dims numbness   When it soothes
which could take them back to sleep
not as forgetting   Forget whispering
Who is my loathed—
& so tightened from certainty they might
mask flattery of standing still
because no one will be made mortal
How young does she look   will be relevant
Bodies standing still named from separation
The answer   The airing & sidewalks
will never be unkempt arteries
Pleasure not only vanishes as fact
Definitely a dissolving
He doubts that by then
Tomorrow   He'll be a splat on history

Bull's Eyes

There is a language for bullfights.
Behind all that padding,
the bullshit of picadores
weighs down their horses,
so those hijos de putas
won't get bucked
stabbing the beast
at the neck.
The bull into the padding,
hanging its head lower,
blood rolling off its tongue.
Cruz lets his sons forget school,
so they don't miss this ballet,
the whoopla leading up to the fight.
Streamers raised, músicos
sharpening tunes, the toros
paraded through the center
of Los Altos.
Cruz teaches his sons
that they too are matadors.
Look me in the eye when I tell you
that men must dress for battle,
polish their shoes, grease their hair.

The Burning Garden

for Josefina

Her hand is steady.
The blade is not at fault,　　slicing.

Tears unnoticed.　　Another layer peeled.
Her eyes comparing the onion's skin
　　to her own.

A tomato stain,　　a cut finger
over the chopping board.

One chile,　　then one,　　two more
becomes a bowl of pico de gallo,

　　　　a bold compromise.

Dolores wears pearls
of sweat around her neck.
　　A furrowed brow.

Sometimes a man is at fault.
One hungry husband and　　his floating

　　　　promises.

For every one of his empty words,
one of the garden's chiles.

Her burning heart.

　　His burning mouth.

When Work, Men Disappear

Here between Los Altos
and El Paso, lines

curve for maps.
The midwife's stare, older. Her
hair, kept long—

ancient strands or hemp
turned white
                    to mark time.

In braids, memory keeps everything
                    close to her body.
                    Midwifery

means knowing blood, crying
lungs pulled into the world

—watching eyes open first.
It means naming the sex,
rubbing foreheads with olive oil,

holding newborns like a mother.

It means announcing
Dolores has given birth to blue
eyes. It means holding the baby

while Dolores watches
Cruz board a train

North—

Dry River, Worn Dress

1.

Without footprints. One side of brick
wall. Her body on the road
leaves perfume and dust   trailing.

The oleander in bloom.
          The poison behind pretty.

Floating white petals.
The devil's winds.

Barefoot beginnings
toward El Norte.

2.

Seashells in the desert,
     a mule's ribs
       jailing the only apple

he has left in his bag. Without water

both take shade
before walking or sleep.

Where stone blocks
stack toward the clouds

—a giant must've
          played here once.

That walk,
     only blurry figures
     in an aura

of silence.

Of soft fabric. The sky,
     bluer. Heads
     fighting to stay up.

3.

What memory?   Distilled
from field grass, hands

running over green blades,
        bending narrow leaves.

Clay walls surround emptiness.
She'll tell you she shared
        her pillow with a rifle

once. On her neck, a mole.
Lunar: of the skin.
A silver necklace of the mines

        strung to a key. Never mind
        what unlocks,
        those strands of cut hair,

        how she used to look.

Alchemy of Space

No particulars.
Comfortable only
        in these moments.

Then not.
Cada minuto:

        My body,
        better seated

then not. A sudden
shift. Out the door.

Sleeping next to a wife
until he didn't.

Listen to song
        skin sings, organs
        make. Cruz

knew when to move,
when leaving was good.

The Men in Saguaro Suits

In the open field, all men talk at once
about guilt. This is a historical feud.
The man with a white brim's tilt slit
my uncle's throat for singing boleros
by an open window. Down in the Barrio
de España, the draft, his voice once alto
with the moon. One man two man
that man four. Sons leave their fathers'
home. Jealousy is a puncture wound
stretched into a smile. No more sons.
That was the year the flood took all
the women's clothes. The washing
rocks, the tall grass where Balvina
learned the skip of stones—

      Hello railroad smoke
      Dancing through the open window.
      Open border cross.

Dragging Daughters

Collected twigs
become people—little dolls
from the broken fingers of branches.

Apricot trees, colored sketches,
scribbled green rows.
Classmates in procession.
One head
peeking out behind a shoulder,
                               nothing in straight lines.

At school, an empty seat,
a name left floating.

No running with friends. Arms
to catch apricots in an apron.
               Her mother tossing stone fruit
          instead of dropping it
into a gunny sack.

          A woman, more than sweat
          from her bandana. Red when working.
Even beneath a tarp of leaves.

Orchards over cotton fields

where other mothers pick and fill,
bodies bowing to the rows—

dragging their daughters on burlap
to the next spot
of dirt, the next bush.

Dolores en Los Ángeles

In the dark, a hand
searches for water.

Thirst carried in glass to sleep.

Dolores when the sun slipped
through the blinds.
Dolores shooing children off her bed.
Covers, wrinkled hands.

San Martín de Porres,
patron saint of animals.
A rosary

of green plastic beads.
One guardian

angel walking boy and girl
over broken planks. Blind faith
over troubled water.

All this watching
Dolores sleep.

In the morning she says
her guardian angel drank
the holy water she left.

She holds the cup,
half-empty for proof.

Grandmother, Curandera

Blood on the upper lip.

        Buckled knees
when the temperature drops.

Little girl.
Little grandma
              with a fix.
Snake oil for the legs.

        A marble on the tongue,
          to hold back bleeding.

With head tilted back,
      a penny between brows
           to be sure.

For future spirits,
an elixir of beef liver and table wine.
In a shot glass,
      not a spoon.

In the garden, hierbabuena.
Little lady pinching leaves
      for a stomach ache.

Drowning leaves
      in a blanket of boiling water.

Counting from the Rooster

The old man opens his eyes.
The first miracle. He makes it
to the mirror. His brown skin,
plowed earth. Regardless, he says,

Thank you, Lord, for giving me—
Another day drips into his palms.

In the kitchen needle pinpoints vinyl,
Jorge Negrete's tongue plucking ballads.
An old mind begins to wander.

The light, a long neck stretching
sun to Tequila bottle.
Illuminated glass. The old man.
Drunken eyes crawling like the hour.

War Flowers

All those sunburnt photographs of Cruz on the wall.
Those camera flashes making blue eyes in black and white
appear hollow. Parachutes in bloom.

In certain photos, people say he resembles Chepe.
All of Chepe's photographs lost in the war.
Tossed into a trunk.
Burned at the Aguascalientes station.

Revolutionaries let sticks of dynamite go.
Time frozen. In a flash, rifles fired from squads.
A fire snaked from one car until surrounding that trunk
of all that Chepe owned.
That fire grew until the photos bubbled like serrano skin.
Clean palates muddled from the burn.

You didn't have to be there to know that fire.
In every photo of Cruz, his eyes,
dandelions before a wish,
blowing through the picture paper.

Breathing Room

Magnolias around the hem,
the weight of their print
repeated. She dreams
of Pittsburg, California,
of growing stems.

Even with her back bent,
turned, she can't walk
away   can't switch
darkness for glass vases.

Remember those eyes,
the darker ring—
          haloed hazel.

Songs without lips
moving. Sunflowers
                    overcrowded
never stem
the height of fence posts
if the roots struggle
to breathe.

Their Eyes Like Dandelion Clocks

I will eliminate more and more . . . neither mouths nor eyes will appear.
—Rufino Tamayo

Behind the lens, a bead.
On the other side,
brothers. Circa 1932.
One toddler's head
beneath an older brother's.

Wink. Shutter.
The two of them
in front of that Ford,

headlights and grill
half-hidden. Childhoods
almost American.

In the same Northern
California where these two
stared into glass.

A glass border
between their faces and the fingers
owned two generations later.
Tracing first with a pulse,
inheritance, replicating with charcoal

the brim of a newsy cap,
a child's tie tucked
gently into his vest.

This still life, not the Model T
driving later across the border
into México.

These charcoal pencils
for the darker parts of history.
Tire shadows. The Repatriation Act.

The lighter parts: fingernail plates,
shirt collars, incisors, two eyes: green.
Two eyes: blue. One camera's flash.

Midnight Crossing

She brought two things on the train.
Her bag and everything that fit inside it.

Lipstick the color of embarrassing
strip searches by border guards,
a medallion of Saint Christopher,
The Prophet by Kahlil Gibran,
a pair of off-white undergarments,
a handkerchief to wipe away depression,

and the drying roots of her violets.
This purple flower is a wetback like me.
This flower blooming in the California winter.
A cluster of rain clouds resting above dirt.

When she is a grandmother, she will tell the story
of migration like this—

PART TWO

Where ink is worn like turquoise stone

Desert Floral

She is two things at once: Human and Fossil.

—Brenda Hillman

Brown skin the seat of memory. Watered from the belly. Faucet I have forgotten.
Twins in a mound of mud before this way or that. Can we privilege the black

hair rivered over the left, before the right cliffs of her shoulders. This way over that.
Take the colors, trails when she leans, her head tilting the sun. One serape. Print mocked.
A long walk under clouds and tears of acid from the mines.

If we bury the children under the juniper tree, string the seeds around our necks
we can ignore the herd, become the skin of a drum, later. Ghost beads and bleating

goats. I am distrustful of their rectangular pupils. Of getting lost near the mountain:
north-trending. Mesa de las Vacas with seams of coal running. Underground stampede.

Stamp us east of sacred lands where resistance is the knotting of a leaky hose,
brown skin at the seat of memory. Watered from the belly. A faucet we have forgotten

when we bury the children under the juniper tree, string the seeds around our necks. Plant huizache. Plant mesquite. Sing of brittlebush and cascalote. Of barrel and of creosote. Of scorpion weed and coral bean. The desert's floral dusting

where my great-grandmother put a marble on my grandmother's tongue, a penny between her brows to damn the river of blood coming down her little nose.

Getting Here

I was chiquita
cuando my parents died.
We must have been rico.
Yo me recuerdo servants
and a big house. I remember
a little brother
pero I can't remember su nombre.
There was a war going on or something.
Era just me and my sis, so we
gave him bread, that's all there was,
pero él no tenía teeth.
And the pan, well, era tan hard
he began to bleed. Pobrecito.

My sis and I fuimos con otros familiares.
A tío or somebody took us
to live in El Paso. See these teeth?
They're American. They were born here.

Sabes que, I can't even remember
what my parents look like.
And I haven't been back to México since.
Tampoco sé what it looks like now.
My father? Se llamaba Valentín.

I must have been fourteen
por hay when I hopped another train.
Los Ángeles was different then, you know?
My sis and I worked
at a sewing factory. Right there
off Broadway y,
cómo se llama? I forget.
Look at my fingers. Mira.

Some weekends my sis and I
used to go hop a red car.
Around then Maria Felix
was on the big screen.

We used to go.
We used to watch esas mujeres
in black and white. That's how
I learned to give my lips color.
Watching those women in the movies.

Lemon Grove Apartments

There's someone, at last . . . who drives you away.
—Rimbaud

Forget about the complex,
the little girl and the busted patio chair
she stands on
watching her mother
and her mother's boyfriend

through their apartment window
—a smaller drive-in movie—

She sees bodies slapped
by blue television light. Wrestling bodies.

To *get lost*, for a couple hours,
means playing with dirt. Other children

stalk the white owl grandmothers warn of.
A tecolote when the sun burns, an omen.

The little girl plays dead
behind the oleander bushes.
She's nameless like the shadows of cucarachas

crawling to cover and confuse
summer's children waiting the onset of dusk.

Street Sweep

From the neighbor: Buster Browns, a party dress.

Watch her jitterbug
the hell out of this broom;
sweep a beige cloud.

Don't look at her
that way. That fist   a rock,
a beating
pulse.

Watch out for clean-cut
boys. Pachucos look deceiving.

They'll steal a drag from a Pall Mall,
a sip of Seagram's. Then
cruise the boulevard.

Her sweetheart has a name—
          pressed inside her skin
          where ink is worn
          like turquoise stone.

Territories

Between lips,
a dormant line,
the San Andreas Fault.
A left-
hand scar
gives up the chisme.

Those fists

belong to East Los,
this side
of the Sixth

Street Bridge.
The L.A. river.
Other girls
know she isn't
playin'.

Pachuco speak:

A switchblade
tucked inside

her pompadour.   A dance
at the Y,
the Armenta Brothers,
hair grease,
distracting shine.
The stiletto in case
her man has beef.

On the street,
Jim Beam cobijas,
Broadway gutters
for pillows.
One cantina
too many.

A mother   and   sewing

factories and Singer
sewing machines.
Who we are.
Who we become,
even with sweet
bread and canela.

Over there, on
the corner
of Whittier

and Bradshawe,
she steps over bolts

of lightning,
as to avoid bad luck.

The webs spiders draw
into sidewalk, give cuentos.

This scar?
Once tattoo.
Once initials
of an old flame.

Stiletto

Flick-knife.   Edgemaster and Shur Snap.   Trademarks. American Soldier.

Telescoping blade.   After 1945. Needle-like point.   Vestigial crossguard.

Optimized for thrusting.   Presto pocket knife.   *The Toy That Kills.*

Woman's Home Companion.   *As any crook can tell you.*   Snake's tongue.

Gang warfare.   Pachuco boogie.   Jealous hands.

Lunar on the Skin

Memo has
José's nose,
the tip
pointing
toward
the ground.

Carlos has
his grandma's
ears.

Alejandra has her
nostrils,
your mother's
lips.

Chuy has
Chepe's dark
black hair.

Chepe's eyes
are with Cruz.

Selina,
she doesn't
look like us.
Her nose
is Roman.
The mole
above her lip
comes from
the moon.

Dream Child

Mom's echo down the street. Collapsed against the magnolia trees—
one in front of each postwar home. *Morales!* against stucco walls in
California's dream of suburbia. Every parked car with an unlocked
door. A window cracked, inhaled my last name. Seat cushions like
lungs suspended in fear. The only one standing on the sidewalk,
studying a roly poly. A gray bead, tucked inside itself. A fetal position.
All of its tiny legs, its fragile belly wrapped inside a soft shell.

Birds without Warrants Arrest the Silence

Hummingbirds come
to pluck their words.
Perch telephone wires,
        iridescent thumbs,
        mocking borders
        between neighbors.

He is safe
        to sit next to
when his lips stay   pressed.
The protracted beast.
Unsteady trigger tongue
pointing hollow
cylindrical speech . . .

(Endless chatter)   clanking
silverware and ceramics.
Teeth and lengua.

Where are the trees?
Leaves carrying disaster   in the wind.

        He will end   in preposition.

        Without searching the hours
        and their mouths

            are dry with promise.

Capped inside mason jars, the long scream,
      the lost toast,
        the love note

        purloined off cellar shelves.

Tainted vino tinto.
Tinted glass birds without warrants
arrest the silence,

the names the sky takes
when the sun is falling.

Minus a Tortilla Press

He was helpless
waiting for the first one—
the moment she slipped it from her hand
to the bed of a towel, gently folding
over the cloth to secure its warmth.
He on the other side of the island stove
with a butter knife licking his lips.

One man standing,
one woman separated by fire.

Instead of that perfect circumference:
the sound hole under nylon strings,
she rolled dough into Jamaica flower
or sometimes cloud animal.
The shape of inexperience.
Before owning a tortilla press.

When the dough was this hot
it formed pockets of air.
Steam whispered
when the tortilla was ready.

She'd press her fingers
against that hot cast iron
so calluses would grow.

Recipe 34. Dismantling

Pulling apart the casings.
That flurry of purple.
Pintos set to dance too long
without enough room.
One ounce of not enough
water boiling within cast iron.

Two more ounces of absorption,
two pinches of cumin and a bay leaf.
A week's worth of sustenance,
a trouble's work imbedded deeply
in the wrappings of my skin.
Sin again, rinse, and repeat.
These are the tastings, a spoonful.
A remedy for home.

Leave it long enough to see
how tradition, grandfathers
cursed when they weren't kissed
sweetly by the last taco's bite.
When a plate is empty, add more.
Leave the plate in the sink
for the man to—
paint himself inside his father.

Gutter Water River

after Roberto Bolaño

Give her a knitted sweater
to pull over her head
when porch heat becomes suffocating.
A buttoned-up shirt
over a pit-stained plain white.

Sometimes she is easily three layers
removed, numbed
like the frostbitten fingers
of a shepherd with poor direction.

If she is that woman, far away from the story,
what can she feel for someone else's cold?

Nothing down her childhood street
except the echoes of name calling.
Only in chaos are we conceivable.

The curb, a canyon cliff
where gutter water rivers
ants on a raft made of magnolia leaf.

Not old enough to know
how important death is,
to understand screaming.

All Souls

Today a napkin crease,
a stain against white floral
patterns, dimpled into soft paper.

Tell me about your people—

Some things are only immaculate once
until we've wiped our lips of mole.
Before she says, *Maria de Jesus,*
her great-grandmother's name,
a stranger asks,

Why is your face painted like a skeleton's?

When a child in a stroller
waves it is because
she hasn't learned
to look the other way,
that she shouldn't stare
death in the face.

Today they are one current.
A dry river running.
Contours molded.
The movement of stillness.

Her hands have become mirrors
of her mother,
her mother's mother,
her mother's—

Don't ask questions,
just fall in line with ghosts.

PART THREE

. . . time was not passing . . . it was turning in a circle . . .
—Gabriel García Márquez

Rocks in My Pockets

In lieu of throwing them through windows
letting air into the old home on Josie Ave,

where an old woman hanged herself
before my parents moved in,

we should hold these rocks and discuss
the storytelling of grown-ups.

I confess, the history of railroads
afflicted more than the women
       who took up rifles instead of staying
       behind to make tacos for one army
                    or another.

Colorful interwar
begins traveling in ever-darker spirals.
The personal tale of family disturbance
reaches back to the story of our grandmothers.

Grandma being discovered
standing in a river,
lacking the weight of rocks
that might help her sink to the bottom.

I inherited drawings,
ripples on mental sheets.
Burdens captured in the repetition of gathering
forty buckets of water every day
to keep the family of papier-mâché
memories a little more scattered—

Gravity in Threes

On ice, a seven-year-old boy dug the blade of his skate—the tip—so that he could spin. The eye of a dandelion must be that flimsy too. If you were that boy or a piece of paper, a nucleus knocked left against its membrane—flesh tucked inside cocoon. Frozen water, not the warmth of piss. Consider a little boy's forehead. A shell cracked. One egg over easy.

March in Los Angeles

The blotted sky
on my mother's face.
The mask of her pregnancy.
The clouds are clearing up, she said.
She never smiled in photographs.
Always hiding her face.

The sky opened.

        Put eight candles on the cake.
        Most birthdays spent pressed like frijoles
        refrying at my grandma's house.

                Beans didn't signal something special.

        Cousins wanted to hide in the tree house.
        Tías wanted kisses, to pinch my cheeks.
        Tíos didn't say shit, tilting their cervesas back.

Both sides of the family came.
My mom's from East L.A.
My dad's from Huntington Beach.

        More people from my dad's side.
        A difference in skin color, too.
        Mexicans with lighter skin and upward noses.

        I was blindfolded,
        spun around eight times, and let go
        with a bat in my hand toward the center
            of assimilation.
        I couldn't see,
            swinging away the air.
            Missing alcoholism,
                disdain for darker skin.

The difference in children:
Some got whupped. Some got talked to.

The piñata bounced and swung—
A papier-mâché donkey tied to a rope
my father held
standing on the fence.

A Son above Ground

Nicknamed *Boo* for half of the mistake
              our parents couldn't erase.

A blunder binding parents together,
the words children don't understand.

Boo video-game-playing, hair bouncing
                     when Kid

Icarus commanded. Boo,
open mouthed.
The sound of his name.

His sudden movements, maybe
the only thing he controlled.

Dad went nights
                without sleep,

dreamed with his eyes open:
a son flying: succeeding at love,
a single moment
         unplanned like
         that one conception.

That Boo made it to twenty-five
higher than all other days,
wearing the fog like a rosary
        around his neck.

Boo on the edge of a roof.

How the Moon

That night the moon became a clock
ticking away the little trust.
Mythology is a goddess's head,
severed by her brother,
tossed into the night sky
when their grandma wasn't looking.

This week's cliffhanger
sounds like Spanglish television.
The steady flicker of blue
her telenovela splashes
across grandma's face.
A reminder for us to stay silent.
Even the phone
with a finger to its mouth.

I chewed gum quietly,
while my sister blew small bubbles.
Our grandmother pointed
toward the drawer
we could find it in—

before sleep, restlessness.
The wall clock has stopped.
It's always 9:52.
Fingers are stuck.
Pointing is second nature.

Even after she tricked me
into eating shit, my sister's face
didn't change. The hard casing
on my tongue turned soft
and without surprise:
only a persistent hush.

Black-Eyed Blues

He'd only hit the wall
around her body.

The holes left
not from strength
but thin wood.

My fists would wilt
if I raised them
at him, father said.

When a bully
left my body bruised
father pointed to St. Jude.

Told me to pray
before school.

My folded hands forced words.
My body waited

for St. Jude, for proof.
Maybe a cloud of smoke,
the bully and his body
folded in half.
But nothing.

A Long Walk, A True Rib

1.

When hands gripped my curls
and slammed my head into the wall,
a dent in white stucco
became a trapdoor.

My eyes marked and remembered
each drenching of sour names,
the thoughtless tongue in a mouth
discarding me like a sponge,
worn from constant scrapings.
Broken dishes in a faded kitchen.

2.

Me on the floor
after seeing the way lips trembled.
After saying *you look drunk*.
After the stumble home from the bar.

Me like ice cubes
crushed and stabbed for a cocktail.

One time the handle on a broom to my ribs.
One of my upper seven.

I always hid under my bed
in my room. To hurt me,
the walk down a long hallway,
passing old family photographs.
Each and every scolding eye.

When the Saint Came Marching

Commonplace: owning marbles
like other boys of seven.
My pal would nod and say *nobody
shoots with their thumb on Thursdays.*

Then came Saturday.

When I was lonely.
I remember the leap
from childhood fear,
breaking up.

Beauty is certainly careless,
its own excuse.

The sun spots like flattened marbles
over the backs of my dad's hands
work around the familiar.

I was sixteen before I
witnessed a human statue for sale.
Processional saints divorced.
We gather those too.

Her amber glass eyes
somehow left me cold.
Carried me six blocks.

Collect something, dad once said.
That is the secret to happiness.
Certain objects miss their own kind.

The Math between Lips

In Mexico, stone kisses:
frog statues at Guanajuato's gate.
Geometry stamped to sidewalks.

The two of us
coaxed by our fathers
to move closer.

Those men pressing folklore
on our backs,
shoulders—*the balcony lovers*
between osculation.

Curvature at the point of contact.
Lips never meeting with mine,
above the cobblestone hallway.
A ten-year curse.

At ten years old I asked God for love—
Painted fairy tales.
I looked to my grandmother.

Bullshit, she said,
when I told her
how my heart felt divided.

Curandera or gutter mouth?
A simpler math:
My grandmother telling me,
Guapos don't cry.
They grab their balls.

Mama Lola

My father said she was part wolf.
Half a woman in a cave somewhere
in Los Altos. Not because buildings
were absent. Not because adobe walls
held her inside the animal of her skin.

That they sang, *La luna ya se metió*
one birthday before she came to live
in the US. One moon in the back bedroom
of a tío's shambled house.

She never wore a smile, he said.
Like happiness could be pinned
over heavy eyes. In a photograph
from her wedding day,
wearing only a starchness in her lips,
a modest dress.

She used to howl, he tells me,
*whenever the moon pressed its face
outside her window, begging her
to recount how old she was,
the lives she'd lived.*

Letting the River

Grandma once counted pebbles
en el rio de San Pedro,
river that was more a creek,
a furrow through the center of town.
She washed laundry against its bank,
tossed away wishes,
breaking the stillness
water held each morning.

She came to stay with us.
I saw her nude, dragging her pants
around her ankles
from the bathroom to her bedroom.
In daylight she pretended
the living room was the plaza back home,
stopping to greet a man,
give in to his request to be married,
to take a stroll around
while the serenata played.

Grandma grew into a little girl
standing barely taller
than the kitchen counter,
wading in the waters of a little river.
Counting pills. Begging for them.
One for sleep.
Baggage.
One for depression.
Laundry.
One for cholesterol.
Her father.
That river.

Behind the Welder's Mask

Grandpa pulled a saw
to destroy what his hands built.

My little head stuck
between wrought-iron fence posts.

This front-yard fence kept me
from running into the street,
from asking about borders.

Most days, grandpa kept
behind a mask.
What the men did
so their eyes didn't disappear.

About that thin line:
The one resting between
blindness and blue flame.

How easily hard surfaces melted together.
Taking risk with every curtain rod,
every bar stool.

The Woman in His Watch

for Brian Lee

Grandpa saw
every face
in muted colors.

Blues blurry, for example.
A softer blend around the frame
of any picture in view.

He listened for time.
All watch or clock faces
turned gray.

Time from a woman's voice
he carried on his wrist.
A watch from the Braille Institute
to his ear. A button press:

The time is eleven o'clock.

He wanted me to ask him,
to hear her voice.
He held the answer close.

> *. . . eleven o three.*

She has black hair, he told me.
The color of funerals.

She looks like this:

The space between paralleled palms.
Invisible.

My grandfather's fingers traced
an outline of *her* silhouette.

To the possibility
in a smooch. A grumbling stomach
remembering when hours war
or the hour before lunch.

Defrosting Curses

While grandma made refried beans
I stood in front of her refrigerator
with both doors peeled open
like a chest cavity. I don't know
what I was looking to remove
when she demanded
I *close the goddamn doors.*

I asked about all the bags
she had stuffed inside her freezer.
She told me it was her compostable food.
Said the trash man appreciated it,
that courtesy,
prolonging the birth of a bad stench.
There were no city composting services in East L.A.
Her yard was all cement.
Frozen garbage, her gift
to Tuesdays. A slower defrost.

Frozen is forgotten.
This week doctors removed her second breast.
Her mastectomy, symmetrical grandmother.

She didn't mourn that breast
even if she *didn't feel like a woman anymore.*

The cold loss didn't make her any softer,
the same curses melted from her lips.

At the Conquistador Hotel

Tijuana, Mexico

I.

Uncle Joe says,
Go meet some women.
Don't come back with bugs.

The ceramic plate,
the refried beans in front of him,
swiped with the last flour tortilla.

Chewing, he waves us off,
communicating, *yes, mis hijos, go.*

On the dusty street, our cab driver whistles.
His seats—covered with woven blankets,
soft acrylic fiber, fading colors,
a coastal landscape, las playas, at sunset.
Postmarked 1998. Meant for Los Angeles,
but rerouted farther south,
past the Bullring by the Sea.

Around the rearview hangs a rosary,
bright-green beads catching headlights.
Golden crucifix squeezed
between the cab driver's thumb and pointer.
Not such a baubling act for a believer,
driver of these treacherous roads,
mustache like Cantinflas.
Our cab driver, minus the fedora,
minus the red bandana around his neck,
or the white henley, asking us finally
where we'd like to go.

2.

His eyes roll in the rearview
when we say, *Rosarito*. His look devours
the notion of a harmless encounter
in that touristy beach city.
A venture away from love
or monogamous girlfriends,
the permission our fathers gave us
to keep loose tongues, freedom
before settling down.

My uncle tells a joke, in Spanish:
An older bull and a younger bull
are standing on a hill, overlooking
cows grazing a field.
The younger bull says, *Let's run
down this hill and fuck the first cow
we see.* The older bull
looks at the younger bull,
looks toward the cows,
and says, *Let's walk down . . .
and fuck them all.*

He told us once
he saw the policía standing on a corner,
next to a quiet, dark street here in TJ;
two dealers took him down
to score some mota.
He said the cop just stood there,
didn't bother. Not even when
a black SUV pulled up and two men got out.
Not even when those men went into a house,
dragged another man out,
blew open his head,
threw the body in the trunk.

3.

On this stretch of coastal countryside,
no mules,
no bulls.

The horses along a creek take tourists
to the beach. We are almost there.

We're leery of the police bribes, of driving
in this country to be pulled over
for a fairy-tale kind of speeding.
If not for the cab driver—

if only there was a button
for "pochos" wanting relief,
to stop without having to
butcher Spanish,

Esta es, uh, bien.

Ah-kee pour fah-vore.

      Grah-see-ahs.

It's nighttime outside La Vaca Loca.
The Crazy Cow's brass playing
can be heard from the street.
We have to remember how to boogie
with manners, how to make popcorn
from hot kernels so that everyone's happy,
making sure not to grind on another man's girl.

No matter how "single" she looks,
there's always a man with a cowboy hat,
in the shadows, watching his woman dance,
a good hand on his gun.

If I could open a window here I would,
if I could let the warm air in—

Between T-Bone and Porterhouse

Blood on my fingers,
woman with a wedding ring.

If a meat saw: bone dust.
Coveting your neighbor's wife.

I finger the filet mignon.
Finger the difference.

Honesty is grinding meat.
She asks politely for a trim.

Lingers a second too long.
Wanting to hold her skirt

steak over my blackened eye.
Will the meat man's lady?

—*Allow me to grab you a fresh cut.*
One with a marbled river of fat.

Behind the door, employees only.
Blood washes toward the drain.

I forget a straight back sometimes
heaving a carcass frozen solid.

To the hook, the hindquarter.
The old-school way.

When She's With Me

Maybe my girlfriend and every man
she meets communicate in secret,
tugging on their collars
to talk to their own bellies—
reverb off roundness.

I draw blue beyond an ocean,
my favorite color too.
But I don't own a drop—azul
in my iris. The hues I burden
are browner. More earth bound,
a head out of the clouds,
chin down.

Her closed eyelids invite
more than blood vessel.
Pockets of red.
In darkness she'll make islands,
sailboats, infidelities.
Make eyes with me.

Let's count the times she shuffles
her feet, turning them concave
inside tennis shoes
while listening to *his* laugh.
The message sent up her legs,
into—
　　　　My hands belong here . . .

What if *his* eyes are the right kind?
She will carry them into sleep,
beyond a blink—

no one taught me this.
But I have learned the signs:
the way she twirls a finger
inside the caramel
of her hair.

The Root of Ugly

On one side, glistening seafood.
Glass vinculum.
On the other, a finger pressed flat.

Quotient between desire and façade,
when the bell chimes,
about six pounds of shrimp.

When I leave for lunch
I am behind another woman.

Under her. A common denominator.
Boredom over emptiness.

Have you seen my girlfriend?
She's prettier than the woman I eat with.
The root of ugly is learned.

Inside my locker, a secret note,
phrases and checkmarks
rating performance,
positions, size.

In the bedroom women's perfume
times stale fish.

Today's special: Bottom feeders.
A week old, but appearing fresh,
spritzed with water, behind glass.

Lovely Little Fucker

The two of us sit like large unopened bandages: Tightly bound fabric strips around a child's folding chair; coiled wire hangers, human armatures.

The contours of guitars and rifles finger the intersection of my words. When belittling ends you're left sheathed in bright-yellow yarn.

I never loved—you lost child: a slow rupture of capillary. A boulder of words to hold on to when you step into the lake.

Winding and unwinding in my head: betrayal. The ritual of flight and fight, of weaving without looms.

Mystery provokes speculation. Tangle me on your tongue. *My lovely little fucker.* Say it like you mean it.

Upbraiding without swords: the mole we both have on our middle fingers give the spider aim to link us. Sudden web of culture. To tangle ourselves inside the confusion of builder's home and death trap.

Silk patterns and solitude, a final product of the loom.
What you kept coming back to: color, texture, swirly adventuring. The codified set of knives
   behind my smile.

Tradition is invalidated by failure. In many ways like the extraction of gin from a cocktail.
   Today I hold images of science. Of nests: you.

Neural wiring. My completed self teasingly visible.

A toast to the great spasms of cruelty punctuating the air we breathed:
the belligerence of impulse, insults, a kiss against your cheek.

Slight: A Requiem

We ended up in Hell.
               Its frosting-thick artifice.
                   Peculiar as it is intense.
But there's no mourning
here. The feeling in the room
               not totally unsatisfying.
                   There is conversation, gunfire,
people second-guessing how
the heart requires more alert viewing than
pantyhose and abstract yarn-wrapped bulbs,
a supply of thread and collection of maps.
                  Everything's fine, she sings.
                   Anywhere but with you.
They say death comes
           to loose tongues.
                   That the bitter and profound
                   rely on light and
                   other inept causes:
                   pockets full of dust.
That we would end
writhing in a tiny space,
an opulent home and its bloody totality
               as ugly as it is beautiful.

               Sequences even more disturbing,
               surely scare the shit out of
                   some couples.
But not all of them.
        Uncertainty is feverishly
        fooled by its appearance.
                 To be pretty
                 she'd tell you, was no simple task.

Staging the Invisible

Tears are liquefied brain.
—Samuel Beckett

Except for the odd *ha-ha* here and there,
a little stream or brook,
you can ghost-read *love me*
into the last (and negated word)
I would like my love to die.
We crave enchantment
even though it makes us gullible.

The etymology of attraction
has to do with the lure,
a song of a fish at the end of a line.

She lives now in a foreign version
of growing together.
Agit ensemble (if we truly grow).
Maybe fleeing east
from the islands of sensibility,
we've pulled ourselves into a lie.
We scoundrels of the world.
Readjusted apertures.
My door remains imperceptibly ajar.

All at once, a foreboding shadow:
staging the invisible.
If the latter is lucky, blessed with an eye,
our lives are endless.
The way a cat is about the house.

Our language consists of silence.
The language of action:
a slamming door, a cup of water to the face.
Silent figures still.

Love is a clumsy retreat.
A dog and a cat sharing a basket.
A caged parrot and a bowled fish,
sharing a tiny table.

Wars arise for lesser things,
to overdo the sign for an undoing.   How many times?
How mathematics helps us to know ourselves.

Acknowledgments

Thank you to Elise McHugh, Hilda Raz, and the University of New Mexico Press for believing in this work.

Thank you to the following journals where these poems, in varying forms and sometimes under different titles, have appeared:
Crab Orchard Review: "Gutter Water River"
Faultline: "Dragging Daughters"
Más Tequila Review: "Dream Child," "March in Los Angeles"
Naugatuck Review: "A Son above Ground"
New Mexico Poetry Review: "Dolores en Los Ángeles," "Grandmother, Curandera," "Mama Lola"
Painted Bride Quarterly: "Getting Here," "Territories"
Suburban Review: "War Flowers"
Supersition Review: "Lemon Grove Apartments"
Volta: "Birds without Warrants Arrest the Silence," "Desert Floral," "A Folkloric Truth," "Lovely Little Fucker," "Staging the Invisible"
Waxwing: "Men in Saguaro Suits"
Willows Wept Review: "Breathing Room"

And thank you to the following journals, who have published other poems of mine along the way:
Acentos Review
Blue Guitar
Crab Creek Review
Furnace Review
Glass: A Journal of Poetry
Hinchas de Poesía
Huizache
Tinderbox

With deep gratitude and affection for my mentors and teachers:
Alberto Ríos, Cynthia Hogue, Beckian Fritz Goldberg, Norman Dubie, Jeannine Savard, Sally Ball, Jack Elliot Myers, Gerald Locklin, J. Michael Martínez, Sharon Olds, Bob Hass, Brenda Hillman, Evie Shockley, Forrest Gander, Charla Howard,

and my first poetry teacher, Velvet Pearson.
I'd like to especially thank the following people:
  Maceo Móntoya, Alejandra Pérez, Jennifer Givhan, Jane Wong,
  Hugh Martin, Katie Berta, Shomit Barua, Christian Perticone,
  Dale Pattison, Dexter Booth, Mark Haunschild, Bojan Louis,
  Allyson Boggess, Natalie Martínez, Chris Emery, Rachel Andoga,
  Sara Sams, Chad Fore, Katie McNamara, Cruz Pérez, Carlos and
  Carlos Pérez, Jacque and Janina Otanez, Justin Brakefield,
  Daniel Mills, Renee Simms, Sean Nevin, Alexa Pérez, Selina Pérez,
  Esteban Pérez, Scott Montgomery, Brian Lee, Brian Diamond,
  Rose Swartz, Kyle Grant Wilson, Eduardo Corral, Oliver de la Paz,
  Rigoberto González, Todd Kaneko, Plynn Gutman,
  Myrlin Hepworth, Austen Johnson, Jolene Torr, Kathy Price,
  Vicky Vertiz, Sa Whitley, Ama Codjoe, Laura Swearingen-
  Steadwell, Bakar Wilson, Stewart Shaw, Magali Roy,
  Emily Jungmin Yoon, Monica Sok, Angela Ina Peñaredondo,
  and Maya Marshal.

Special thanks and recognition to the following programs:
  Arizona State University Creative Writing Program
  Arizona State University Young Adult Writing Program
  Arizona State University Young Writers Program
  California State University, Long Beach Creative Writing Program
  Community of Writers at Squaw Valley
  Long Beach City College Creative Writing Program
  The Prague Summer Program

To my parents, ancestors, and extended familia, whose lives and stories
have become the nuggets of folklore and legend.